# Mindful Classroom Design

*A Guide to Creating an Ideal Condition for Teaching and Learning*

By Bee L. Medders

Cover Design by Matthew Legaspi


ISBN:1548836435

# Contents

**ACKNOWLEDGEMENTS**

*No man is an island.* This title of Thomas Merton's book certainly captures our need for others in our lives. Without the following people, this book would not have been written.

First and foremost, I would like to express my deepest gratitude for my family especially my husband Mark and my daughter Lauren. Thank you for listening to me talk about writing this book for years. Your encouragement to keep at it made me believe it could happen.

Thanks to my nephew Matthew Legaspi for designing the cover and my nephew Lukas Forsman for helping with the graphics. To my second cousin Candice, a special acknowledgment. I bet you never thought your comment that day you came to visit would make an impact in the lives of teachers and students. Thank you for asking the question, "Are you into Feng Shui?"

To the board members of the Alameda County Reading Association, especially Dr. Sybil Hoffman, for twisting my arm to do a presentation on room environment using practical principles of Feng Shui and to Lori Oczkus, who planted the idea in my head to write a book about how to set up a classroom, thank you all for giving me the confidence to share what I have learned.

To all my colleagues and friends, to those who attended my workshops, and those who allowed me to work with you on your room environment, I am truly grateful. Special thanks to Neena Barreto, Ruby Dellamano, Viviana Espinoza, and Cheri Benafield.

To Tina Bobadilla-Mastel, Summer Journey Frost, and Robert Guarino, thank you so much for editing. Your valuable time and expertise were greatly appreciated.

I would also like to acknowledge Kitty Dixon and Dr. Adria Klein for their support and positive influence in my professional life.

To you, the reader, for your interest in learning how to create a classroom that is inviting, safe, and a happy place to teach and learn, thank you for giving me a purpose for writing.

Last but not least, I would also like to express my gratitude to all my students and their families. In my teaching journey, I learned how to love learning and to be kind to myself and others. Thank you very much for the privilege of having been your teacher.

May peace, hope, and love be with you always!

## INTRODUCTION

A school is a place to learn. It is important to be mindful of that.

There are many books on what students need to learn, how students learn, and methodologies for teaching. *Mindful Classroom Design* is about noticing what is in the physical space of a classroom and creating an ideal condition for teaching and learning.

Have you ever stood in the middle of the classroom, looked around, and noticed how it made you feel? In his book *The Energy to Teach*, Donald Graves stated, "Yes, there are approaches to teaching that we need to know about but they take second place to the conditions for learning. You, the teacher, are the most important condition in the room." A teacher's sense of well being is very important. One reason why I wrote this book is to help teachers be mindful of their health and happiness. Healthy, happy teachers are good for students!

Have you ever asked students how the classroom makes them feel? It is one assessment rarely, if ever, that is given to students. Is the classroom inviting, and does it make students feel welcome? When a kindergarten class visited a first grade classroom, one little boy said, "It feels happy in here. I'm going to ask my mom to put me in this class next year." The kindergartener's feedback confirmed that students are affected by the classroom environment. In *Teaching Essentials*, Regie Routman posits about room environment. "A beautiful and comfortable well thought out space can impact our sense of well being and our desire to learn and work". This book offers step by step suggestions on how to make a classroom comfortable, aesthetically pleasing, and inviting. A friend and colleague who attended my workshop on room environment texted me to say, "I think about how this idea makes my classroom a better place. In my case, my students' lives can be so stressful that a classroom becomes a haven." I hope this book will assist teachers in creating a haven for all students to learn and thrive.

What makes this book unique? Most books on education draw solely on years of research. This book not only draws on research but also on ancient wisdom and plain old common sense. Often, intuition is neglected to inform decisions. Our body tells us what we need. We just need to be still, listen, and then take action. Keep in mind, the *invisible* internal feelings affect the external environment and the *visible* external environment affects the internal feelings.

As you apply the suggestions offered in this book, remember be present in the moment and make every moment count. There is a saying, "Yesterday has passed, tomorrow has not happened, today is a gift. That's why it is called present." Unwrap, discover, and use the gifts you have been given since the day you were born. Ultimately, my hope is that in the process of creating an ideal condition for teaching and learning, teachers will feel empowered and enjoy the journey of living healthy, happy lives every day to make a difference in the lives of students. What is education for if not to learn how to live life to its fullest. Inhale, exhale, and be grateful for the breath of life!

# Part 1: Use of Space

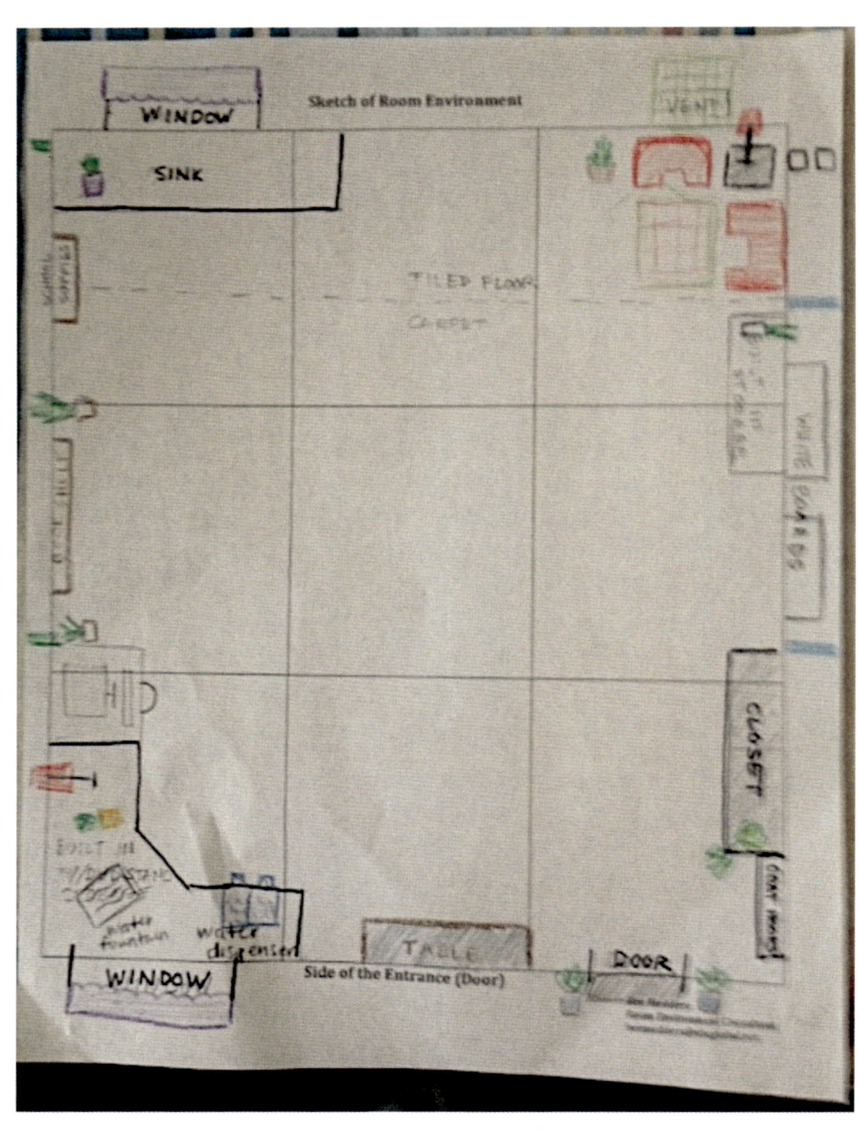

## FIRST STEP: ASSESS

Start by doing a self assessment of the classroom using the Self Assessment Continuum. The items to assess on the continuum typically contribute to what makes the room look and feel undesirable, functional, or ideal. Fill in the bubble next to what is true for you. Do not think too hard and just go with your gut feeling. Completing the assessment first will give you an overview of the current state of the classroom. Is it mostly leaning towards undesirable, is it somewhat functional, or is it in an ideal condition?

This book is organized by topics that address the items on the continuum so you can go directly to the section you need. Part one is about use of space and arranging the furniture. Part two is about creating a clutter free, organized, and inviting classroom. Typically, clutter is a major culprit of what makes the condition for teaching and learning look and feel undesirable. You might consider reading the decluttering section as a top priority. If you're a new teacher or veteran teacher just setting up a new classroom, this section can help you create a clutter-free environment from the get go. Part three contains anecdotes, research, and background knowledge on Feng Shui for your information and rationale for the suggestions in this book.

After assessing, you can determine the area or areas to focus on. Choose ONE if there is more than one area that is not yet in an ideal condition. Trying to tackle every item that you marked undesirable can be overwhelming. When you feel overwhelmed, the typical reaction is to just ignore the problem and keep pushing harder to make students learn. I would suggest trying to address an area that is functional and make the necessary adjustments to make it ideal. By tackling a manageable task and seeing immediate results, you will feel energized and inspired to continue tackling undesirable items in your assessment.

Remember, you are the most important condition for learning. Do not let the environment control you, instead, you control the environment. You will feel empowered when you have a sense of control. You might even begin to notice all the things within your circle of influence. If you feel stuck or feel a sense of helplessness, you will feel energized and inspired to continue tackling undesirable items in your assessment. It will change your attitude about your ability to make the changes you want to see. It might be a small step but it has the potential to create a "butterfly effect," a term coined by Edward Lorenz for the concept that small causes can have large effects. Whenever you are feeling like things are out of your control, you may want to reassess.

If you are just setting up the classroom, you can use the continuum as a guideline for things to keep in mind in order to attain an ideal teaching and learning condition. For the first couple of weeks of school, I take the time to stand back and just observe how students are moving in the space, especially during transitions. I watch to see if students are able to access what they need, where the "trouble spots" are, and make adjustments. The more students can independently take control of their own learning, the less time you will need to manage behavior issues caused by the physical environment that take time away from teaching and learning. Investing time in creating an environment where everyone is set up to succeed will pay off high dividends in the long run.

## SELF ASSESSMENT CONTINUUM

**Directions:** Fill in the bubble next to what is true for you. Do not think too hard and just go with your gut feeling.

| Notice | Undesirable | Functional | Ideal |
|---|---|---|---|
| **When I enter the room I feel…** | ○ Unmotivated to teach<br>○ Unprepared<br>○ Anxious | ○ Ready to teach<br>○ Somewhat prepared<br>○ Somewhat relaxed | ○ Energized to teach<br>○ Well prepared<br>○ Calm |
| **Air Quality feels…** | ○ Stagnant<br>○ I'm suffocating | ○ Some circulation<br>○ I'm surviving | ○ Good circulation & flow<br>○ I can breathe freely |
| **Furniture Arranging** | | | |
| **Furniture Arrangement** | ○ Does not feel good<br>○ Impedes movement, poses safety issues<br>○ Time consuming for students to enter, exit, and transition | ○ Works<br>○ Students can move around safely<br>○ Time for entering, exiting, and transitioning varies | ○ Feels welcoming<br>○ Allows for safe movement<br>○ Minimal time used for entering, exiting and transitioning consistently |
| **Student Desks** | ○ Makes collaborative discussion and group work challenging<br>○ Spacing poses safety issues or/and contributes to behavior problems | ○ Arrangement can be adapted for collaborative discussions and group work | ○ Arrangement easily allows for collaborative discussions and group work |
| **Classroom Library Arrangement** | ○ Not well defined | ○ There is a designated area for books | ○ Designated area is inviting and comfortable |
| **Decluttering** | | | |
| **Teacher Desk** | ○ Serves as a clutter catcher and looks like a disaster area | ○ Has mixture of necessary and unnecessary items | ○ Clean with only necessary items on top |
| **Window Area** | ○ Serves as a clutter catcher<br>○ Light blocked | ○ Catch some clutter<br>○ Partial light shines through | ○ Free of clutter<br>○ More natural light enters the room |
| **Organizing and Labeling** | | | |
| **Top of Cabinets** | ○ Stacked with boxes and/or miscellaneous disorganized items | ○ Has miscellaneous items somewhat organized | ○ Clear with healthy plants |
| **Classroom Library Organization** | ○ Books are not organized in any particular way | ○ Somewhat organized in a particular way | ○ Books organized and labeled by themes, genre and/or levels |
| **School Supplies** | ○ Not accessible to students<br>○ Precious time used to pass things out | ○ Somewhat organized and some items labeled<br>○ Students need assistance accessing occasionally | ○ Organized, labeled, and have designated places<br>○ Accessible to students without assistance |
| **Items Stored** | ○ Disorganized<br>○ I use up time to locate what I need | ○ Somewhat organized, some things labeled<br>○ I can usually find what I need | ○ Items in designated place, organized, and labeled<br>○ Easily accessible |
| **Decorating** | | | |
| **Walls** | ○ Covered with commercial posters and/or outdated charts with faded background<br>○ Items unused by students<br>○ Looks disorganized and lack any color scheme | ○ Mixture of commercial posters and class generated chart from current and previous lessons<br>○ Some items students use<br>○ Colors mostly bright | ○ Contain charts from current lessons<br>○ Items support students to take initiative of own learning and self regulate<br>○ There is a sense of order<br>○ Colors emit a sense of calm and balance |

## FURNITURE ARRANGING

Learning is a social event and a well thought out furniture arrangement can facilitate opportunities for various interactions. Arrange furniture to allow space for whole group instruction and discussions, collaboration in small groups, as well as a space to work independently. Before moving the furniture around, follow the time and energy saving steps below.

### STEP 1: Sketch

Draw a sketch of the layout of the room. Label the door(s) and windows and draw any other non-movable items such as the sink, built in storage, and shelves. An example of a typical classroom layout and permanent fixtures is shown in Figure 1.

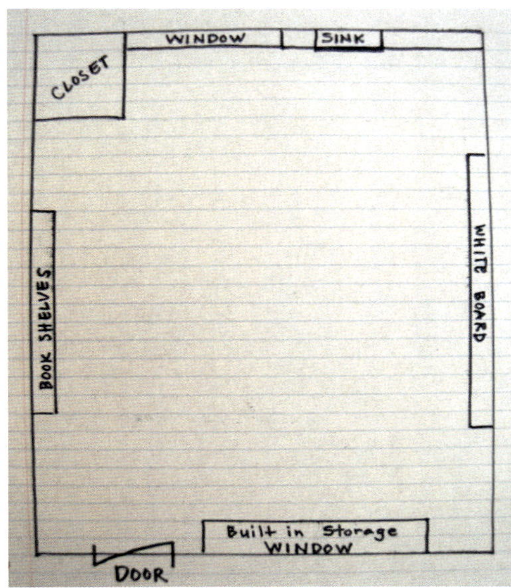


**Figure 1**

### STEP 2: Decide

Choose a teaching wall where whole group instruction would take place. Ideally, this wall is large enough where you can hang chart papers and pocket charts. Typically, teachers choose the wall where the whiteboard or smart board is located. If students will be sitting on the floor facing this wall, like in most primary level classrooms, make sure there is enough floor space for students to sit with enough elbow room.

With Whole Group Area determined, next decide where tables for Small Group collaborations will be located and how they will be arranged. Also, include where the teacher might work with a small group. At the primary level, there is typically a designated table for small group instruction. If you have single desks or double seating desks, you will have to decide on the configuration to create table groups.

## FURNITURE ARRANGING

Avoid rows and columns. Classrooms are already full of straight lines and edges. In the decorating section, I will explain the concept of yin and yang to create a sense of balance. Arranging the tables to add more straight lines make for an overly yang classroom. Tables could be arranged to create curves in order to balance the energy in the room.

Arrange tables or groups of desks around the whole group area so students can see the "focus wall" from where they are sitting. At the primary level, there are times when whole group instruction is necessary while students are sitting at their desks. This will save time transitioning from small group area to whole group area. Figure 2 shows an example of one configuration.

**Figure 2**

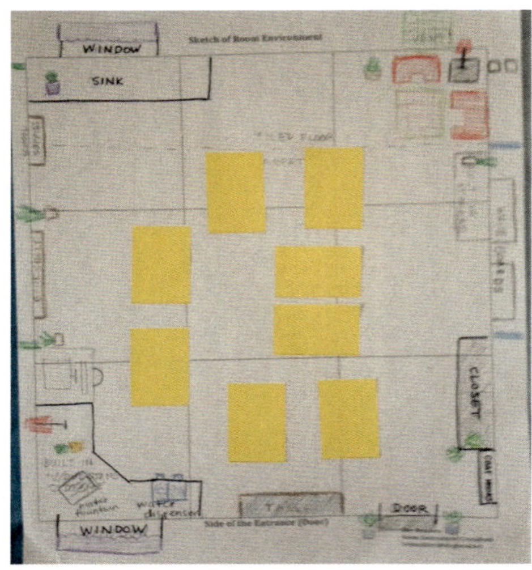


---

**Tips:**

- Use post-its to play with different arrangements
- Use the whiteboard to sketch classroom layout and arrangements

---

If you have space, create a Quiet Area. It is ideal to have a classroom library or an area where students can read or work independently. Some rooms can accommodate a couch for a cozy and comfortable area for reading. Pillows on the floor to sit on can also be used to give the room softness.

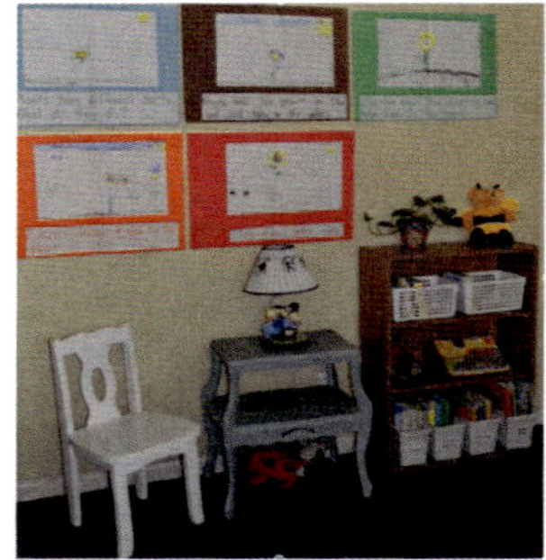

In early primary classrooms, I would recommend having designated areas for the various activities students will be engaged in and where the materials to be used would be stored. I suggest having a Writing Area, Science Area, Math Area, Art Area, Listening Center Area, Computer Area, and a Playhouse or Dramatic Play Area.

## FURNITURE ARRANGING

### STEP 3: Move

Now that you have a plan, it is time to start moving the furniture. Be careful not to hurt your back. Invest in furniture sliders. Get help for super heavy items.

As for the teacher desk, if it is serving as a clutter catcher, you might consider getting rid of it if you can. It frees up floor space for student use. If there is a table for the teacher computer, make it also serve as a teacher's desk. If you must have a teacher desk, ideally position it so you do not have your back to the door. There is an element of surprise that keeps the teacher on edge whether you are aware of it or not.

Once you have arranged the furniture, you may have to make a few adjustments. Even a slight angle or a few inches here and there can make a difference. Test for safety. Make sure when students slide their chairs they will not be hitting anything or anyone behind them. Check also for flow of traffic. Make sure there is enough space for students to walk around and in between tables.

For the first couple of days of school, stand back and watch how students move around the room. Assess for areas that cause congestion. Assess if arrangement allows for easy transition from one activity to the next. When I am coaching teachers, I often time how long it takes for students to transition. Time is what teachers often say they need to reach all students. This is where you can gain minutes.

One class I observed took a minute to transition from whole group to small group instruction while another class took five minutes. Imagine saving four minute times the number of transitions a day. Multiplying that by the number of school days in a year adds up to a whole lot of minutes. When you do the math, you can see you can gain a lot of time for teaching and learning by being mindful of your furniture arrangement.

The teachers I observed were equally dedicated, passionate, and experienced teachers. One difference was their room environment. One teacher had attended my workshop and applied the principles I offer in this book. The other teacher was open to making changes. After we worked on her room environment, she reported it was taking less time for her students to transition. Even if you save a minute or two just by rearranging the furniture the minutes add up.

## FURNITURE ARRANGING

Here is an example of a classroom arrangement after applying the steps. These photos were taken from a fourth grade classroom.

Whole Group Area

Groups of desks are arranged for small group collaboration around the whole group area giving students visibility of the teaching wall from where they are sitting. At the far left corner is a semicircle table for small group instruction.

# Part 2: An Inviting Classroom

## DECLUTTERING

Decluttering is one of the most important steps. It will not matter much what you do to the room environment if you skip this step. Here is why.

Clutter is a silent culprit of negative effects. I repeat, clutter is a *silent* culprit. You have to slow down and observe how it is making you and your students feel. One day a teacher shared with me that a troubled student told her, "I need order in my life." Although he was not referring to the classroom environment, she looked around and noticed how there was no order in the room. The student's comment motivated her to start decluttering. In the process, the teacher reflected on her own need for order.

**Negative effects of clutter include the following:**

- **Drains energy:**
  How do you feel when you see your teacher's desk piled with tardy slips, student work, forms due, parent notes, dry erase markers, paper clips, binders, confiscated items etc.? It can make you feel overwhelmed and like everything is out of control. Clutter induces stress especially when you can't find what you need, like your lesson plan or the worksheets you just made copies of during your lunch break.

- **Wastes time:** Looking for things uses up valuable time that could be better spent doing constructive things.

- **Wastes money:** When you can't find what you need, it is easier to go out and buy it in order to receive instant gratification. Not only will you end up wasting money on items you already own, but you will also have to buy containers to store unused items you misplaced the year before adding to the unnecessary clutter you should be trying to avoid.

- **Safety Hazards:** Boxes and other items on the floor or above cabinets are potentially dangerous. You can prevent tripping accidents by eliminating clutter on the floor. Avoid storing heavy items above cabinets that can fall during an earthquake or hurt your back when taking them down.

- **Makes cleanup difficult:** Custodians tell me they love cleaning my room because they can easily maneuver their vacuum cleaners. They can get under desks and tables when the floor is clear. They can wipe the counters and clean the sink. They confess how in some rooms they are unable to clean thoroughly because they are afraid to knock things down or simply can't maneuver their vacuums due to all the clutter.

- **Attracts pests:** Dust mites, cockroaches, and mice love to take residency in undisturbed spaces to hide and reproduce. Clutter cultivates an environment where pests can thrive.

## DECLUTTERING

Here's a photo of spools of strings where mice had nested. This photo was taken by a teacher who was decluttering a closet of her new classroom that she inherited from a veteran teacher.

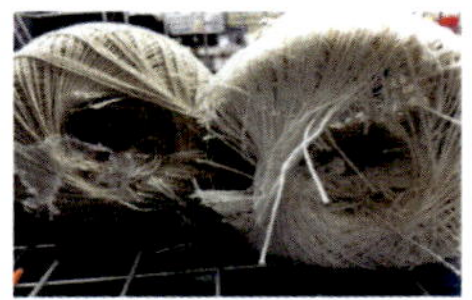

Before going on to address clutter issues, I would like to offer a common definition. Clutter could be defined as anything useless that is taking up valuable space. For example, obsolete and broken items are typical clutter materials taking up space. Clutter could also be anything that is making the room look disorganized and chaotic. Useful things that are mish mashed or misplaced can make the room seem cluttered. By mish mashed, I mean unrelated things all thrown in the same container or area. For example, magnets, post-its, paper clips, dry erase markers, and art supplies stored on a chalk rail. By misplaced, I mean items in places that are not typically considered or used for storage. A common example would be books and boxes stored under a teacher's desk, papers all over the place, and school supplies in random places could also make a room look cluttered.

### How to Declutter

Here is an easy system for decluttering: choose one area, a closet, a shelf, or container depending on how much time and energy you have each time to declutter.

**Sort items into 4 piles:**

**Pile 1: Keep** – these are things you use daily or on a regular basis

**Pile 2: Throw away** – anything broken, obsolete, or no longer serves a purpose

**Pile 3: Give away** –things you no longer use but others might need

**Pile 4: Hold** – items you think you might still need or have difficulty parting with

**Tip:** A good idea to help let go of items taking up valuable space but has sentimental values is to take a photo.

## DECLUTTERING

In an article, "Everyday Mindfulness Exercises for Stress Relief," Elizabeth Scott writes, "Because clutter has several hidden costs and can be a subtle but significant stressor, cleaning house and decluttering as a mindfulness exercise can bring lasting benefits. To bring mindfulness to cleaning, you first need to view it as a positive event, an exercise in self-understanding and stress relief, rather than simply as a chore."

If you feel like your classroom is draining your energy, you are wasting time and money, materials are hazardous, you have custodial issues, or pests are attracted to your room, the solution is simple: declutter. When you feel like you have control over something, it is empowering and empowerment can be energizing!

---

What Decluttering the Top of Cabinets Can Do

**Before**

**After**

Decluttering the top of the cabinets not only makes the library look more inviting, but it also makes it safer. In places where earthquakes are common, large and heavy free falling items on top of cabinets are potentially dangerous. Keep safety in mind.

# DECLUTTERING

## Clutter Prevention Strategies

**To maintain a Clutter-Free Environment**

- Have a place for everything.
- Keep everything in its place.
- Label, label, label!

- **Touch it Once**
  This tip is typically for items that clutter the teacher's desk.

  **Junk Mail** - Most schools have mailboxes for teachers. One thing that helped me from bringing clutter into my classroom that usually ends up on top of my desk is to look at the items in my box and sort right then and there. Any "junk mail" goes right into the recycling bin next to the mailboxes. If you don't have one, get one. You'll not only free your room from unnecessary papers, you can also help save the earth.

  **Papers Needing Your Signature** – Keep a pen in your box. Sign anything that needs to be signed and turned in to the school secretary on your way to the classroom whenever time permits. Giving yourself a few minutes extra before the bell rings to check your box will save you a lot of time in the end. If you're like me, I often misplace the papers that need my signature and I spend my prep period stressing out and looking for the piece of paper that got buried under all those catalogs and flyers.

  **Catalogs** - Have a bin for catalogs by your door and place them as you enter so you don't bring them to your desk or end up setting it down somewhere else cluttering other areas of the room.

## DECLUTTERING

Remember, have a place for everything. For the flyers and notes that need to go home, I have a bin labeled Outgoing Mail. Everything that I need to send home with students goes in that bin. I save so much time searching for these items when it's time to send them home. Also, if you have a parent helper who can put these things in the students' mailboxes or cubbies, as they are referred to in the early primary, they know exactly where to look and know what needs to go home. My school had a communication envelope that went home every Thursday, so I had a parent or student helper put the items in the outgoing mail in the envelopes. Once you train a parent or student to do this, you won't have to supervise freeing time to do other things like analyzing student work or preparing for the next day. If you can do the work at school, you won't have to do these things at home. You can relax, get reenergized, and be refreshed for the next day.

Maintaining a clutter-free environment is a way to keep the clutter from taking over.

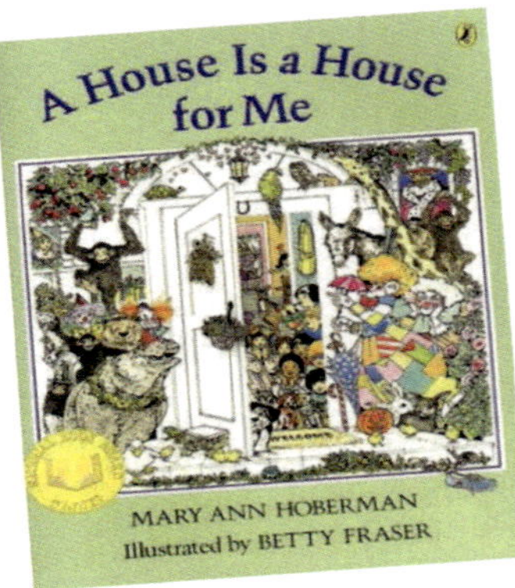


*A House is a House for Me*
by Mary Ann Hoberman

This book is a good read aloud to teach everything has a place. When something is left on the floor or misplaced, I ask the students to please help find the item's home.

*Example: A garbage can is home for trash.*

### Clutter Accumulation Prevention

Here is a tip especially for new teachers: be selective when kind-hearted veteran teachers are giving "stuff" away. Bring in the room only what you need in the moment. You will save a lot of time and money from trying to store these items you may never ever use.

## ORGANIZING

After clutter is discarded, it is time to organize and put like things together. Our brains are always looking for some kind of order. Start by sorting teacher materials from student materials and keep them separated in different functional areas of the classroom.

Take curriculum materials such as teacher manuals and other resource binders and place them in one area such as a bookshelf. Preferably, put teacher materials in the area where you do your lesson plans. Having what you need at your fingertips can save you time from walking back and forth.

A before and after photos of bookshelves taken in a middle school classroom demonstrate how organizing can make a difference. Separating the teacher's materials from students' materials clearly distinguishes what students are permitted to access.

**Before**

**After**

Notice how the area of the room looks more like a library rather than a disorganized storage area.

Store student materials where they can easily be accessible. Put like things together. This is especially helpful in the primary level. Put daily school supplies like sharpened pencils, crayons, colored pencils, scissors, etc., in one area. Use a bookshelf or a counter to store items. (Examples can be found in the Labeling section.)

## ORGANIZING

Consider designating different areas in the room to store content specific materials. Below are examples of storing and organizing materials based on content.

**Classroom Library:** In interior decorating, you will hear decorators talk about having a focal point in a room. If we want students to love reading and learn the importance of literacy, consider the classroom library as a focal point of the classroom. When organizing, think about a system that will not only support students in retrieving and returning a book but also one that supports and reinforces the curriculum. Figure 3 is an example of how the room environment can support students in meeting standards.

**Figure 3**

| Standards | Environmental Response |
|---|---|
| **Reading Standards for Literature Grade 1**<br><br>**Craft and Structure**<br><br>Explain the major difference between books that tell stories and books that give information, drawing on a wide reading of a range of text types. | Library organization<br>• books that tell stories<br>• books that give information<br><br>Create a chart together and list characteristics of books that tell a story. Hang it in the classroom library where books that tell a story are stored. Do the same for informational text. |

**Writing:** You might have a table or shelf for items students need to complete writing assignments. Different papers, writing tools, staplers, and resources for writing could be in a designated Writing Area.

**Science:** You could have a Science Area for materials used in Science. Often, some math materials like rulers and balance scales are also used during a science activity. Combining these two content areas or putting them next to each other would be ideal.

**Math:** Materials used for math could all be stored in the Math Area.

---

**Tip:** You might store books about math concepts in this area if you have additional shelves.

---

## ORGANIZING

### Organizing Books

This photo was taken from a fourth grade classroom where most of the books are paperback chapter books. The teacher organized and labeled them in baskets and tubs. Notice how she grouped similar containers together giving the library a more orderly look.

Here is an example of books organized according to reading levels.

**Tip:** The teacher intentionally chose the color green as a matte for labels because her library was located on the East side of the room. You can find further explanation for the reason in the decorating section.

Books organized by genre or topics.

## LABELING

Once items are sorted, organized, and placed in their designated areas, it is time to label. It takes time to label but it pays off in the long run.

There are different ways to make labels. If you can afford a label maker, I recommend getting one because it is worth the investment. Label makers are good for labeling small items, files, drawers, and cabinets. To label large items, I use the computer or make hand written labels and use packaging tape to adhere those labels onto items; It is nice and clear and easy to remove without causing damage to classroom furniture.

Some teachers involve students in labeling the room. It is a purposeful way to teach phonics in the early primary grades. Identifying items in the room that start with a particular letter and writing them interactively is one way to generate labels. The only caution I would advise is to be sure student-generated labels are spelled correctly and letter formations serve as good models. After all, what we see over and over will be imprinted in our brains.

Start by labeling items students use daily such as pencils, crayons, scissors, glue sticks, and markers. Work your way around the room labeling items in each of the areas in the room. Get items you will need the first day of school labeled first. Sometimes, if you start with decorating the bulletin boards, you run out of time to do these the little things that will help make the day run smoothly. Think about the procedures for retrieving and returning the materials and calling attention to the labels. It also helps to label the spot where the item should be placed. This provides support and guidance for younger students to successfully put things back where they belong. In the early primary level, matching the labels becomes a purposeful word matching game.

Other benefits of having things labeled include serving as a "dictionary" for spell check and as a "flash card" for repetitive exposure. Some students bring the labeled item to their desks to copy or they go over to the area where the items are stored to support spelling words correctly. When students know how to help themselves, you will not hear them say, "How do you spell?". Labeling objects such as the door, flag, clock, sink, paper towel, and soap dispenser also helps support English Learners. Use the environment strategically to serve as your partner teacher to support students. This is one example of working smarter not harder!

## LABELING

Labels support English Learners

In addition, you can hang signs from the ceiling, if it is low enough, to label areas. If you think of the classroom as a large file cabinet of information, labels help students retrieve what they need quickly. If students can navigate through their environment independently, then the teacher can focus her energy and time on assessing, instructing, and facilitating learning.

Example of signs hanging from the ceiling

When you have labeled items students need, label teacher materials and items stored in the cabinets and drawers. For example, keep all types of papers in the same cabinet, any art related supplies in the same storage unit, and teacher resources on the same shelf. You will save time looking for things if there is a designated place for items in the same category.

Organize and label for the same reason grocery stores, automotive stores, and other retail stores organize all items they sell and that is to help customers find what they need without assistance. A classroom where students can learn how to help themselves is ideal.

## LABELING

Prioritize and do a little bit at a time to make labeling a less daunting task. If you stay in the same room year after year, you really just have to do it once. Until labels start to fade or you need to change locations or containers, labeling would not be something you would have to do every year. Once it is done, you will find that the time spent is worth the investment. You will save a lot of time and it will teach students how to be responsible for their environment, take ownership of their own learning, and self regulate.

An example of how to organize school supplies for easy student access.

Labeling supplies helps maintain organization. The shelves of supplies also serve as a word bank.

Books used to teach writing.

## DECORATING

When it comes to classroom decorating, how do you make a classroom inviting and promote a sense of well being? How do you decide what colors to use? Where do you place items like a file cabinet or an aquarium? This is when I draw on an ancient Chinese wisdom or the Art of Placement known as Feng Shui to guide my decisions. I simply took the basic principles for promoting health and happiness and applied them to the classroom. If you are curious about how I stumbled into this ancient Chinese wisdom, I included the story in the section Anecdotes. It may sound unconventional, but I like to think of it as innovative!

Before applying the principles of Feng Shui, you may want to skip to the section Background on Feng Shui. There are many books on this subject. I included a few in the reference section that helped me to understand and apply the principles.

### Balance

To promote a sense of well being, balance is probably one of the most important things to have in life. Any time anything is off balance, problems arise. For healthy living for example, we know how important it is to eat a balanced diet. Too much or too little of anything the body needs can make you sick. To maintain financial health requires balancing the checkbook. Balancing is a continuous assessing and adjusting task. If balance is important, what might a balanced classroom environment look like and feel like?

The basic guiding principles of Feng Shui helped me to balance the energy in the room. In physics we learned energy is a property of objects, transferable among them via fundamental interactions, which can be converted in form but not created or destroyed. We know from elementary physics that everything is made out of matter. All matter has energy. Energy is force. Feng Shui offers how to balance the energy in a given space. Notice there are scientific correlations to what the Feng Shui masters observed. Perhaps, if they had been called scientists instead of Feng Shui Masters, the western world would readily consider their findings research-based.

If you want to balance the energy in the room, consider the list of yin and yang that I have compiled from various resources. Energy is invisible to the naked eye and yet humans are receptive to the energy. Have you ever walked in a room when two people have just had an argument? You cannot see the energy it produced but you can feel it. The same way when you rub two objects together, it creates friction. Friction produces heat. Heat is energy. Heat sometimes is desirable and other times undesired. If you keep this in mind, the concept of yin and yang will make sense.

## DECORATING

### Yin and Yang

To create a balance, let us take a look at the two forces, the yin and the yang. Note, one is not better than the other. This is a very important concept to keep in mind. It is about creating a balance between the two forces. Their interaction creates positive energy called chi. Refer to the chart below when assessing the balance of energy in your room. Items bolded are ones to consider to create an ideal classroom condition.

| Yin | Yang |
|---|---|
| **female** | **male** |
| mother | father |
| inner | outer |
| north | south |
| winter | summer |
| down | up |
| matter | spirit |
| earth | heaven |
| negative | positive |
| night | day |
| **dark** | **light** |
| **quiet** | **noisy** |
| **cold** | **heat** |
| **soft** | **hard** |
| wet | dry |
| receptive | creative |
| shadow | sunshine |
| meek | aggressive |
| **small** | **large** |
| **ornate** | **plain** |
| **horizontal** | **vertical** |
| **curved** | **straight** |
| **rounded** | **sharp-angled** |
| **floral** | **geometric** |
| **plants** | **rocks** |
| **odd number** | **even numbers** |

Notice the items in the yang column are those typically found in classrooms. Balancing the number of girls and boys is a common practice when forming classes. Do you know what happens in a classroom full of boys? You get yang energy. Have you heard a teacher trying to quiet a class by shouting above the students' voices? It only creates more yang energy. In classrooms, you will find mostly hard, straight, plain, sharp-angled furniture. These are all under the yang column.

## DECORATING

Typical classrooms are filled with yang energy. To create a balance, we need to consider bringing in items from the yin list. Soft, ornate, rounded, floral, plants, and odd numbers are often missing in classrooms particularly in upper grade classrooms. If a classroom is full of ornate borders, dark colors, and floral designs, the recommendation would be to consider balancing the energy with items from the yang list.

When it comes to balance, think of Goldilocks. She did not like the porridge that was too hot or too cold. Instead, she ate up all the porridge that was just right. We want our students to "eat up" what we have to offer. Instinctively, it seems our bodies desire balance. Have you ever wondered if students feel the imbalance of our institutionalized environment? How might the imbalance be affecting their behavior? How is it affecting you?

## The Balance Guide

When making "decorating" decisions, refer to the Balance Guide designed for classroom use. As mentioned in the Three Major Concepts of Feng Shui there are three schools of thought. I am using the dragon door school. In this school of thought, the **door or main entrance** determines the **north** side. This is important to note to help you determine what colors to use, shapes to consider, and what items to place in each area of the room according to Feng Shui specifications. You will also see that each side corresponds to a cardinal direction. The north, south, east, and west side corresponds to the four basic elements in nature. North is water, east is wood, south is fire, and west is metal. In the center is earth. For example, if you have a fish tank or bowl, it would be ideally placed in the north side of the room. (A rationale and elaboration on the concept of creating a creative cycle is found in the section Background on Feng Shui.)

---

**Tip:** To remember the colors, label the sides of the room with the cardinal direction mounted on construction paper specified by the Balance Guide (example, south written on red paper). Use the signs to teach and apply cardinal words for giving directions. For example, instead of directing students to face the door, you could say, "Would everyone please face north."

---

## Application

Take the sketch of the classroom and divide it into nine sections to help align it to the Balanced Guide. Start with colors. Then, use the guide to determine placement of items in the room according to Feng Shui specifications. Use the Element Table that shows the elements, associations, and classroom examples to assist you.

## DECORATING

### Element Table

| Elements | Associations | Classroom Examples |
|---|---|---|
| Wood | Trees and plants<br>Wooden furniture<br>Paper<br>Green<br>Columns<br>Landscape pictures | Paper tree<br>Real plants<br>Borders with plant designs<br>Bookshelves |
| Fire | Sun symbols<br>Candles, lights and lamps<br>Triangles<br>Man-made materials<br>Sun or fire pictures | Picture of the sun<br>Lamp<br>Borders with triangles or sun designs |
| Earth | Clay, brick and terracotta<br>Cement and stone<br>Squares<br>Yellow, orange, brown | Terracotta pots |
| Metal | All metals<br>Round shapes<br>Domes<br>Metal objects<br>White, gray, silver and gold<br>Coins<br>Clocks | Staplers<br>Scissors<br>File Cabinets<br>White Dry-Erase Board<br>Clock |
| Water | Rivers, streams and lakes<br>Blue and black<br>Mirrors and glass<br>Meandering patterns<br>Fountains and ponds<br>Fish tanks<br>Water Picture | Fish bowl/aquarium<br>Border of clouds, water drops<br>Picture of water scenery<br>Table water fountain<br>Black Borders<br>Sink<br>Water dispenser |

If a permanent fixture, like a white board, is not in the ideal location, don't worry. Much of Feng Shui is about giving you control over things that seems out of your control. A mindset that I have developed as a result of learning about this ancient wisdom is that when I am confronted with a problem, I automatically think, "What are some possible solutions?" This way of being is one I try to model for the students. Whenever a problem arises, I have them think of some possible solutions to address the problem, choose one, and give it a try. If it doesn't work, try another solution. In Feng Shui, solutions are thought of as cures or remedies. (Cures or remedies can be found in the Tips and Tidbits section.) For every problem there is a possible solution. When there is something in the environment that is considered "unlucky" you have control. I like the idea of making my own luck and not leaving it to chance. In addition, intentional, rather than incidental or accidental choices, will increase the probability of having an ideal condition.

## DECORATING

### BALANCE GUIDE

**Focusing on Colors:** *Use to determine colors on the walls/bulletin boards*

| | | |
|---|---|---|
| Purple | **SOUTH**<br>Red | Pink |
| **EAST**<br>Green | Yellow | **WEST**<br>White |
| Blue Green | Black | Gray |

**NORTH** *(Determined by main entrance/door)*

**Focusing on Elements:** *Where to ideally place items*

| | | |
|---|---|---|
| | **S**<br>**FIRE**<br>*Lamp*<br>*Red Items* | |
| **E** **WOOD**<br>*Books*<br>*Wooden Shelves*<br>*Tree (Picture/Real)* | **EARTH**<br>*Terracotta Pots* | **METAL**<br>*White Board*<br>*Computers* **W**<br>*Metal File Cabinet* |
| | **WATER**<br>*Sink, Aquarium,*<br>*Tabletop Water Fountain*<br>**N** | |

**Focusing on Shapes**

| | | |
|---|---|---|
| Rectangle | **S**<br>Triangle | Square |
| **E** Rectangle | Square | Round **W** |
| Square | Free Form<br>**N** | Round |

## DECORATING

**SOUTH**

ELEMENT: Fire COLOR: Red

**EAST**
ELEMENT: Wood
COLOR: Green

**WEST**
ELEMENT: Metal
COLOR: White

**NORTH**
ELEMENT: Water
COLOR: Black

Sink in ideal location.

## DECORATING

**PEACE CORNER**

Mindfulness teacher and coach, Neena, incorporates a Peace Corner on the Southeast side of the room.

Soft blue pillows, purple sachets, and a plant bring yin energy into the space: soft, quiet, receptive, meek.

It is intentionally placed in the area that represents the aspect of life - Wealth and Fortunate Blessing.

COLOR: Purple

---

Friends and colleagues, Viviana and Ruby, texted me this selfie holding the Balance Guide while shopping for decorating items over summer vacation. Good idea to have to refer to.

Notice how happy they are! Imagine the positivity that must have transferred to the students.

---

## DECORATING

### Plants and Air Quality

In addition to using plants to balance the energy to create an ideal teaching and learning condition, it has other health benefits. Adding plants to a classroom décor' is one way to purify the air and improve air quality.

Research done by the U.S. Environmental Protection Agency and NASA concluded certain common house plants improve indoor air quality. They serve as natural air purifiers to remove toxic chemicals like formaldehyde. (For more details, go to the Research section.) Here is a list of recommended indoor plants:

- Areca Palm
- Mother-in-Law's Tongue
- Money Plant
- Peace Lily
- Florist's Chrysanthemum
- Spider Plants
- English Ivy
- Red-edge dracaena
- Elephant-ear philodendron

Spider Plant

If you don't have a green thumb like me, I found spider plants and philodendrons are easy to care for. I water once a week and if I forget, they are very forgiving. You might be wondering why not cactus plants since they require less watering and do well indoors. According to Feng Shui, cacti are considered unlucky. Common sense will tell you why they may not be ideal especially around children.

Note, the agency recommends stop buying products with toxic chemicals. Products like air fresheners fill the air with nasty chemicals that harm your health. As an alternative, fill a spray bottle with water and a few drops of natural lavender oil. It makes for a wonderful air freshener. It is also very calming. If you eat oranges for lunch, save the peel, put in a bowl, and use as popperie. Students comment how good the room smells.

We cannot see the air but it is all around us affecting how we live in our space. The Feng Shui masters may have called these plants "lucky" for a reason. It makes good sense to breathe clean air to promote good health. A healthy teacher can only be good for students. No offense to substitute teachers but less sick days for the teacher means more days of effective teaching for the students. Little things can make a big difference. Plants are one of them.

## DECORATING

One day a colleague asked me to take a look at her classroom environment. Although her classroom was free of clutter and organized, she expressed it did not feel good. She did not feel energized to teach when she entered the classroom. In addition, she did not feel comfortable sitting at her desk. Since clutter was not an issue, I assessed her room for balance. We looked at the Balance Guide to make the adjustments. We focused on the colors, placement of furniture, and items on the walls.

Below are before and after photos of the southeast area and south wall. This is the wall you see as you enter the room. In the before photo you will notice how she chose blue to decorate this wall. According to Feng Shui specification, red is the ideal color on this side. Take note of the positioning of her desk and the bookcase placement. After making the adjustments, she reported she felt so much better being in the classroom.

**Here were my recommendations:**

- Remove the blue decoration of a butterfly and the daily schedule both mounted on blue paper and the blue calendar pocket chart from this wall.
- Use the wall to display the students' self portraits and use red corrugated borders to frame the bulletin board. Conveys the classroom is student centered.
- Remove the bookcase against the desk to create a better flow and angle it to give a wide angle view of the entire room when seating behind her desk. This positioning conveys a commanding stance and a sense of control.
- Change the borders on the bulletin behind the desk to purple as specified on the Balance Guide for the southeast wall to enhance the aspect of life fortunate blessings.

BEFORE AFTER

# BALANCE GUIDE

| | | |
|---|---|---|
| Southeast<br>Wealth/ Fortunate Blessings<br>PURPLE<br>Shape: Rectangle<br>Number: 4 | SOUTH<br>Fame / Reputation<br>RED<br>Shape: Triangle<br>Number: 9<br>Element: FIRE | Southwest<br>Relationships<br>PINK<br>Shape: Square<br>Number: 2 |
| Health / Family<br>GREEN<br>EAST<br>Shape: Rectangle<br>Number: 3<br>Element: WOOD | Self<br>YELLOW<br>Shape: Square<br>Number: 5<br>Element: EARTH | Creativity/ Children<br>WHITE<br>Shape: Round<br>Number: 7<br>WEST<br>Element: METAL |
| Knowledge<br>BLUE GREEN<br>Shape: Square<br>Number: 8<br>Northeast | Career/ Life's Path<br>BLACK<br>Shape: Free-form<br>Number: 1<br>Element: WATER<br>NORTH | Helpful People/ Travel<br>GRAY<br>Shape: Round<br>Number: 6<br>Northwest |

**Entrance Wall (Door Determines the North Side)**

## TIPS AND TIDBITS

### Storing Seasonal Items

Examples show labeled boxes serve multi purpose: a word bank and to keep seasonal item organized for easy accessibility.

### Wall Space Saving Idea

**Word Bank Binders**

Anchor charts and word banks that support students take up wall space, and as a result, teachers often run out of wall space. One solution is to store word banks in a binder. Here is an example of a student using a binder of contraction words. The class can keep adding throughout the year without taking up more wall space.

Other Word Bank Binder Ideas:

- Compound Words
- Verbs/Past Tense

---

To organize and store small items for easy accessibility, use a storage unit found in hardware stores.

---

## Displaying Art Work

**Located on the South Wall**

**Apsect of Life:** Fame and Reputation
**Color:** Red

### Star of the Week Bulletin Board

The Star of the Week creates a Me-Doll. The class brainstorms adjectives to describe the person. Then, the class interactively writes sentences using the adjectives. This serves as a model. As a Literacy Center, students can write a page for the Star of the Week's book.

**Located on the North Wall**

**Aspect of Life:** Career
**Color:** Black

Put a slit in the middle, on top of a 12 x 14 black construction paper and use a tiny clothespin to hold student work. This makes it easy to change out artwork throughout the year. It saves time from stapling and removing staples.

### Credibility

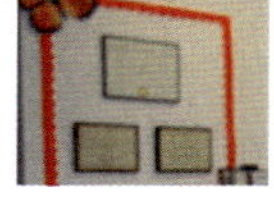

Hang diplomas, credentials, and awards ideally behind the teacher's desk for the same reason doctors and lawyers display their diplomas in their offices. It communicates you are a qualified professional teacher.

### Lighting

If you get migraines like I do, it may be triggered by the fluorescent lighting. Turn off lights if you get enough natural light from the windows. Use wide spectrum light bulbs for lamps. They are good for the brain.

## TIPS AND TIDBITS

### Cures and Remedies

**THE RELATIONSHIPS OF THE FIVE ELEMENTS**

| ELEMENT | Helped by | Harmed by | Weakened by | Weakens |
|---|---|---|---|---|
| Wood | Water | Metal | Fire | Earth |
| Fire | Wood | Water | Earth | Metal |
| Earth | Fire | Wood | Metal | Water |
| Metal | Earth | Fire | Water | Wood |
| Water | Metal | Earth | Wood | Fire |

To understand cures and remedies, refer to the table above. Take the element and determine if you need to enhance or diminish its energy.

Below are examples of common items on the wrong side based on elements on the Balance Guide and suggestions for a cure or remedy.

| Problem | Reason | Remedy | Rationale |
|---|---|---|---|
| White board in the east side | Metal cuts wood | Place lamp or add any red items | Fire melts metal |
| Sink in the south side | Water puts out fire | Put wooden items or use green colors | Fire helped by wood |

---

Here's an example of how these tools have been applied to a principal's office.

Before After

# Part 3: For Your Information

# ANDECDOTES

## My Introduction to Feng Shui

One ordinary day, my brother and I were discussing how a side chair should be positioned in a room he was redecorating. A second cousin, who happened to be visiting, overheard my suggestion. I said, "Place it at an angle." The cousin asked, "Are you into Feng Shui?" I replied, "FUNG WHAT?" To make a long story short, I was intrigued and went on a quest to answer my question, "What is Feng Shui?"

I learned about Feng Shui by reading, almost obsessively, books on the subject. I must have read at least 50 or more books. I now own more than a dozen books. I also researched the topic on the Internet and read many articles. I checked out videos at the library and even attended a mini-workshop given by a famous Feng Shui master who was a guest on a popular talk show. I found it quite difficult to implement what I learned to my entire house. Seeing as the principles could also be applied to an office, I took the simple and practical principles that made sense and little by little applied them to my "office" my classroom.

So, an ordinary day turned into an extraordinary series of events. As I continued applying more and more of what I learned, word got out. The Board Members on my reading association twisted my arm to do a workshop for teachers at our mini conference. I overcame my fears of being laughed at and losing my reputation as a legitimate staff developer and agreed. Lori Ocskus, who happened to be our keynote speaker for the conference, popped in during my session. At the end, she came up and encouraged me to write a book. That was about fifteen years ago.

Since then, I have collected anecdotal data to show how combining the principles from this ancient art of placement and what we know from our own field of education could help make classrooms comfortable, inviting, efficient, and ideal for teaching and learning.

Here are just a few anecdotes or qualitative data, if you will, to inspire you to use the simple and practical principles of Feng Shui that have been carefully selected to help teachers create an ideal condition for teaching and learning.

**Anecdote 1:** In June 2002, a kindergarten class came to visit my classroom to experience a day in first grade. A verbal, uninhibited young boy shouted, "It feels happy in here!" My class looked at him as if what he felt was a given. That was the first year I started applying a few simple principles of Feng Shui in my classroom. I watched this little angel work diligently with joy and enthusiasm as he completed the given task. I knew then there had to be more to his comment than meets the eye. As the class was leaving, the little boy said, "I'm going to ask my mom to put me in this class."

**Anecdote 2:** One day, a colleague stopped by my room and said, "I love coming in here. There's so much to look at and yet there's such a feeling of calm."

## ANECDOTES

**Anecdote 3:** Every now and then my former students would come by during recess or after school. One time, two boys came by. Looking around one said, "It feels like there's air in here. You can breathe." The other said, "I think the ceiling is much higher." I doubt that since our school was a two-story building and I was on the first floor and their classroom was just down the hall. I wondered, "Did they feel like the ceiling in their room was closing in on them and made them feel like they were suffocating? How does one even begin to factor these comments in a research study to quantify the effects of the classroom environment on student achievement?" I thought the difference must have been so noticeable they couldn't help but verbalize what they noticed. Students notice. We just don't ask what they notice. I love it when students feel safe to make comments and give me feedback.

**Anecdote 4:** A teacher, I was mentoring, and I decluttered and rearranged her classroom during winter break. The following week when the students came back, I asked the students what they thought about the new arrangement. One boy said, "It feels clean." Another said, "It makes me feel smarter." I thought, "Wow!" I didn't expect to hear that. Noticed they expressed feelings and not how it looks. The teacher and I just looked at each other and smiled.

**Anecdote 5:** Another incident you really can't justify with numerical data happened during a parent teacher conference. A parent came for a parent teacher conference the day *after* it was scheduled. She entered the room, short of breath, and asked for a more suitable chair for a woman her size. She sat down and began listing defensively why she missed her appointment. I held my breath waiting to be accused of something I didn't do or should've done. She paused as her eyes toured the ceiling and panned her surrounding. Suddenly, she asked in her hoarse voice while grasping for air, "Is this my son's classroom?" I replied calmly, "Yes it is." Then surprisingly she said, "It feels *happy* in here! It reminds me of when I was a little girl." The rest of the conference was nothing like I had imagined from what others had described. Every now and then during the conference she would smile and say how much she liked the room and how it makes her feel happy. As she was leaving I told her she was welcome to visit the classroom anytime. For the rest of the year, she was very cooperative. She returned my phone calls and signed papers that needed her signature. Without giving any excuses or blaming anyone, she gladly paid for a lost book. I believe her positive attitude towards school must have contributed to her son doing well that year and meeting grade level standards.

**Anecdote 6:** One afternoon when the Corp Yard manager was making his rounds, I happened to be in the classroom. His unsolicited comment made me think I have got to share what I know. He told me my classroom was the best classroom he has seen around the district.

## ANDECDOTES

**Anecdote 7:** Teachers who have applied the principles have shared similar stories and reactions from people who come into their rooms. I have included two of the emails I have received over the years.

*My friend Karla and I had such a wonderful time at your workshop, you did a wonderful job. We smile and giggle every time we see each other and ask "How's your chi today?"*

*I moved classrooms early in the school year so I started with the clutter in my file drawers and condensed from 3 - 4 drawer very full cabinets to 2 - 4 drawer cabinets with room WOW did that feel good*

*I have worked to place all the "right" colors and items according to the bagua, except I am still in search of a phoenix. My family has been shopping with me and my little Feng Shui workbook as I searched for the perfect dragon, dolphin, wind chime...I even had a new student find a white tiger for me after I told him about my Feng Shui class, another new student and his parents noticed the environment and were full of positive comments, and the neatest comment came from a new art teacher for our school...who did not know about my Feng Shui class, she entered to set up for her class, paused to look around and said "I really like the way your room feels." all I could do was smile and say thank you as I thought to myself...the chi is positively flowing in here* 

*Thank you so much for your wonderful insight. You did a great job presenting...there is soooo much information out there. I hope down the road you would consider coming to our school and sharing. If you need pictures or a room to share, I'd love to share (although it is a work in progress.) Sorry for the long email, but I can't say enough good things about your class and this ancient art. Sorry, I can not make it to the workshop but I do hope to see you again soon. Well, Have a great day!*

*Ann*
*3/4 Grade Teacher*

*Hi Bee! Thank you for the message...*

*Also, I wanted you to know that I love my room!! I used the Bogwa (spelling?) and love the results. The other day, a fellow teacher was sitting in my room and she said, "I don't get it, our rooms are the same size and we have the same amount of desk, and everything, but your room feels so much bigger to me!" haha, I told her about your class I took and how much it helps to have the clutter gone and more organized. I love it!*
*I was wondering, would the same Bogwa work in my house? I noticed recently that I called my classroom "home" a few times now, and I think it is just because it feels to much more put together than my actual house now. I want to complete my house, setting it up, so it feels good too. Thoughts?*

*Thanks!!!*
*Erin;)*

## ANECDOTES

I remember a time when I kept to myself what I had discovered. Like I mentioned earlier, when word got out, I found myself giving workshops, consulting with individual teachers, and even rearranging my principal's office. I have learned sometimes achievement gaps are created when one classroom has something good students are getting while others do not have access to that good thing. An ideal teaching and learning condition is one of those good things.

Implementing the practical principles from this ancient wisdom has taught me to look beyond the surface and bring to the conscious level an awareness of what we can do rather than focus on the things we cannot do.

*Not all of us can*
*do great things.*
*But we can do small*
*things with great love.*

*Mother Teresa*

# RESEARCH

---

*"I did then what I knew how to do. Now that I know better, I do better." Maya Angelou*

---

Learning more information can help us make better decisions. The following working knowledge of various topics provide some rationale for applying the practical suggestions in this book.

### Working Knowledge of the Brain

What do we know about the brain? Every teacher should have a working knowledge of the brain. How we set up the environment, design our lessons, and interact with students will be more effective if we know how the human brain works. In addition, knowing how the brain works will tell us why certain practices are not conducive to learning and may be counter productive.

### Anatomy and Physiology of the Brain

### The Triune Brain

The brain can be divided into three sections based on their function. They are called the neocortex, the limbic system and the brainstem or reptilian.

The **Neocortex** is responsible for making decisions and judgments on incoming information. It is the "executive branch" of the brain that regulates abstract thought, foresight, hindsight, and insight. This is the part of the brain that makes language and computing possible.

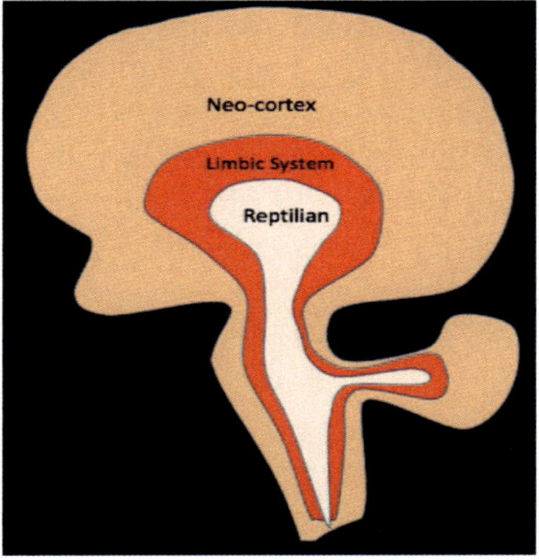


The **Limbic System** houses the primary center of emotion. It regulates homeostasis and controls survival functions (fight or flight response). This part of the brain plays a critical role is the storage of information in long-term memory.

The **Brainstem** or **Reptilian** regulates basic life support systems such as the circulatory and respiratory systems. It governs instinctive behaviors such as establishing territory, grooming, and forming groups.

# RESEARCH

## Implications for Teaching

Emotion and learning go hand in hand. They cannot be separated. In her seminar, How to Teach so Kids Will Learn: A Look at the Developmentally Appropriate Brain, Pat Wolfe, presented the following:

*1. Incoming sensory stimuli are relayed to the neocortex through the brainstem and limbic system. These lower systems strongly influence what we pay attention to and/or find important.*

*Emotion and cognition cannot be separated. Memory is impossible without emotional content. The material we are teaching must have meaning for students.*

*2. Under stress, we experience what Leslie Hart calls "downshifting". We revert to more primitive behaviors; our responses are more automatic and limited. There is less capacity for rational and creative thought.*

What is the implication for teaching and the environment we set up? For the neo cortex to efficiently operate, a non-threatening environment is essential and material must have meaning for students. Sometimes, the threat is perceived rather than actual. In classrooms, the threat is often not physical but emotional. Students could be afraid of failing or being made fun of.

For example, when my daughter was in kindergarten, she came home and said she did not want to go to school anymore after the first week of school. When I asked why, she told me there was a chart in the room that was scaring her. She was referring to a behavior chart. When you misbehave, you change the color of the card that represents the level of infraction. I told her to ignore it and just do her best to follow directions. She said the chart was hard to ignore because it was right next to her desk. The following day when I dropped her off, she sat down at her desk, looked at me, and then pointed to the chart.

If emotion drives attention, and attention drives learning, be mindful of what goes on the walls. I discourage using precious wall space to display charts that students could see as forms of public humiliation. Creating an ideal learning condition is first and foremost fear free. An emotionally safe place to learn is where students can thrive.

University of Southern California neuroscientist Mary Helen Immordino-Yang notes, "It is neuro biologically impossible to build memories, engage complex thoughts, or make meaningful decisions without emotion." On that note, we want to make sure that the school experience students have will be one of pleasant and happy memories.

## RESEARCH

### Working Knowledge of Air Quality

An article posted on Dec. 27, 2013 from the website Mind Body Green Healthy Child Healthy World reported, air pollution inside your home or office can be worse than the pollution outside. The U.S. Environmental Protection Agency ranks indoor air quality as one of the top five environmental risks to public health. To clean up the air indoors, the agency recommends stop buying products with toxic chemicals. Products like air fresheners fill the air with nasty chemicals that harm your health. Researcher Kamal Meattle discovered three common houseplants that improve indoor air quality. They are Areca Palm, Mother-in-Law's Tongue and Money Plant. The Money Plant removes formaldehyde and other volatile organic chemicals from the air.

NASA conducted a clean air study where the results also suggested certain common indoor plants may provide a natural way of removing toxic agents from the air, helping neutralize the effects of sick building syndrome. It compiled the first list of air-filtering plants as part of its study published in 1989 which researched ways to clean air in space stations. Peace Lily, Florist's Chrysanthemum showed removing all of the following toxic agents benzene, formaldehyde, trichloroethylene, xylene and toluene, and ammonia. Other air-filtering plants include: Spider Plants, English Ivy, Red-edge dracaena, and Elephant-ear philodendron. The list can be accessed at Wikipedia NASA clean air study.

### Working Knowledge of the Psychology of Color

According to Saul Wagner in "Classroom Colors Make a Difference," "Numerous studies have been conducted over the years on the effects of color on a person's psychology and physiology, and researchers agree that color definitely has both a mental and physical impact on a person."

### Working Knowledge of Cultural Differences

From the website Learn NC, Bridging the differences: Cultural background of Mexican students entering U.S. schools, Mary Faith Mount-Cors wrote there are differences between school in Mexico and schools in the U.S. One difference regarding environment she noted is this:

"Sensory overload: The tendency in the United States to cover walls and available spaces with learning aids creates an overabundance of stimuli for a student from a spartan school in rural Mexico."

# BACKGROUND ON FENG SHUI

## Working Knowledge of Feng Shui

### What is Feng Shui?

Feng *(pronounced fung)* means wind and shui *(pronounced shway)* means water. Wind and water are the seen and unseen forces of nature. Keep in mind air and water are vital to sustaining life.

Feng Shui originated in southern China some 3,000 years ago. It was born out of the necessity to determine the best and most auspicious places for their homes, altars, and burial grounds. Only recently has it made its way into Western culture.

It has been defined as:

- an Ancient Chinese Art of Placement
- the Chinese art of arranging furniture and homes to encourage wealth and health
- the art of designing your home (and work-place) to promote success in life, health, wealth, and happiness
- the study of how to arrange your environment to enhance the quality of your life
- a system for arranging your surroundings so they are in harmony and balance with nature

### Basic Principle

Our surroundings affect us and we can change them to promote health, wealth, and happiness. Now, wouldn't it be a great educational goal to make our world a happy and healthy place starting with our classrooms? Regardless of the definition, the goal of applying Feng Shui is to create an environment that promotes positive energy.

### Three Major Concepts

One major concept is the flow of chi. Chi is the energy that links all things in the universe. The energy you take from your environment influences your moods, emotions, physical energy and over time, your health. Feng Shui reflects the way chi energy moves. Chi has also been defined as the breath of life.

Another concept is balancing the yin and yang. Yin and yang are two basic forces in the universe that are opposing yet complimentary halves of a whole and their interaction creates chi. They are complimentary rather than competing with each other. In other words, one is neither considered good or bad. Creating a balance of these forces is the heart of the practice of Feng Shui. (See list of Yin and Yang in the decorating section.)

## BACKGROUND ON FENG SHUI

The third major concept is about the interaction of the five elements in nature: Water, Wood, Fire, Earth, and Metal. The creative cycle shows how the elements sustain each other. The destructive cycle shows how the elements can dominate each other.

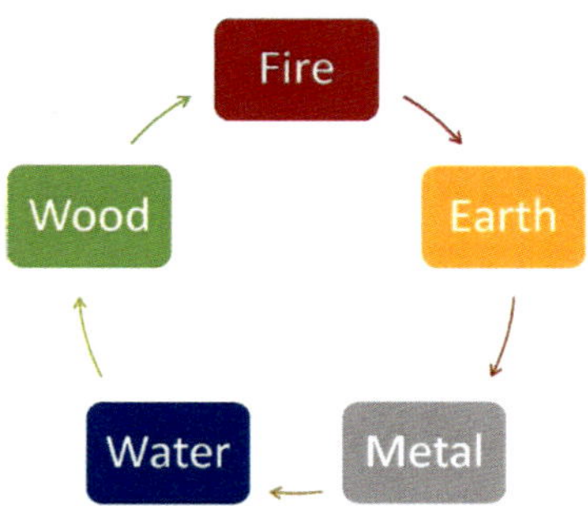


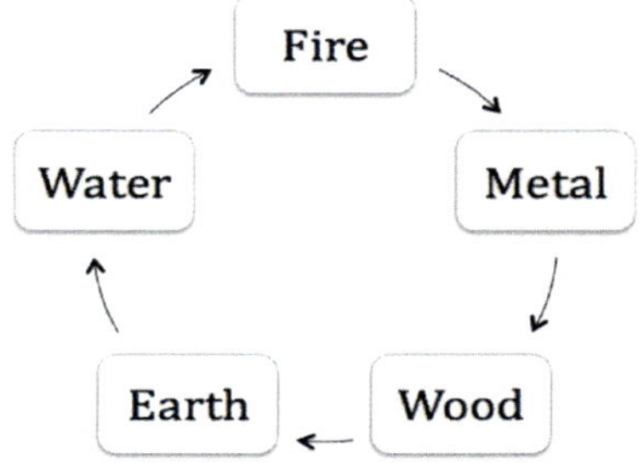


*Wood fuels fire; fire produces earth from its ashes; earth produces metal (ore); metal creates water from condensation;, water nourishes plants and trees creating wood (Ex: use green butcher paper in the east and trim with black border)*

*Water puts out fire; fire melts metal; metal cuts wood; wood takes nourishment out of the earth; earth muddies the water. (Ex: avoid putting a water feature, like an aquarium, in the south area of your room)*

### School of Thought

There are three basic schools of Feng Shui. One is the Form School that deals more with the shape and focuses on the lay of the land. As teachers, we have very little control of where schools are built so I didn't spend time learning about this school of thought. Another is Compass School and this is a more scientific method for finding the right directions. This school concentrates on compass directions and uses the compass called a luo pan and some mathematical prowess. I found it to be too complicated. The third one is called Dragon Door. This school of thought focuses on the existing position of doors and has been adapted to suit modern Western ways. It also makes use of intuition. This is the school of thought I am using in this book. I found it to be the easiest to understand and the guiding principles I have adapted for the classroom will make application simple and fun! Fun! Now there's a word that needs to be part of education.

### The Bagua

To achieve a balance, a tool called a bagua is used in Feng Shui. A bagua is an eight-sided figure with each side corresponding to an aspect of life. It helps to determine the element (water, wood, fire, earth metal), the color, the shape, and the number suited for each area of a house or room. Baguas also traditionally incorporate numbers and animals although these elements aren't necessary to create an ideal classroom.

## BACKGROUND ON FENG SHUI

I have adapted the tool for classroom use and will call it a ***Balance Guide***. I have found Feng Shui as an untapped wisdom where the guiding principles could be easily applied to the classroom to create an environment that softens the impact of educational environment, organize classrooms to minimize lag and management time, and support the curriculum. Student performance can be greatly influenced if they feel welcome and comfortable. They will be eager to enter the classroom and you will too!

Do not let the name Feng Shui for this ancient art of placement deter you from applying its practical principles. I wish I could come up with a more "academic" term so it can be readily accepted in our academic world. People have expressed that Feng Shui is quite complicated. It is also misunderstood. It seems to suggest a bit of superstition because it talks about luck. If you look deep enough, like I did, you will find scientific research to back up what the Feng Shui masters of long ago discovered by observing nature. The law of nature is not biased towards anyone. It applies to everyone. I think that is why the principles are timeless and applicable to any environment – home, office, even classrooms. I have carefully selected practical principles from this art of placement and combined them with the knowledge I have gained from years of experience setting up classrooms and creating an ideal condition for teaching and learning.

If we want students to be innovative, teachers have to be innovative. To be innovative, you have to be willing to investigate outside familiar territory for untapped solutions. In medicine, they call resorting to familiar treatment, familiarity diagnosis. In *Smart Thinking*, Art Markman talks about causal knowledge. When we are stuck in explaining what is the cause, we are able to identify our knowledge gap. There seems to be a knowledge gap as to why some classrooms feel good and others do not. This body of knowledge has filled in some of the gaps for me. While it is somewhat an unconventional practice in schools, the results have been ideal.

Shakespeare said, "What's in a name? That which we call a rose by any other name would smell as sweet." Call it the art of placement, practical guiding principles for classroom decorating, or eastern ancient wisdom meets western modern thinking. Whatever you call it, applying the principles will have a significant impact on your well being.

### Aspects of Life

The Feng Shui masters figured there are eight aspects of life that contribute to the overall well being of a person. An imbalance in those aspects of life creates unhappiness and misfortune while a balance creates happiness and wealth. Mahatma Gandhi said, "One man cannot do right in one department of life whilst he is occupied in doing wrong in any other department. Life is one indivisible whole."

## BACKGROUND ON FENG SHUI

The Balance Guide can also help you to be mindful of the aspects of life.

- **North** represents career.
  If you have a good job, you can afford the basic needs - food, shelter, and clothing. When your basic needs are met, you are more likely to be healthy. With health, you can support and take care of your family.

- **East** represents health and family.
  Being healthy is essential to enjoying life and a family gives us stability.

- **South** represents fame and reputation.
  When people see you in a positive light, it makes you feel good about yourself.

- **West** represents creativity and children.
  In each one of us, there is a natural longing to use our given talents to create something to contribute to the world. Part of the creative desire is to procreate and preserve the human race.

As you look at the other aspects of life represented on the Balance Guide (bagua) knowledge and self-cultivation (northeast) wealth and fortunate blessings (southeast), relationship (southwest), travel and helpful people (north west), you will notice these aspects also contribute to the overall happiness and well being of one's life. Being mindful of each of these aspects of life can help us assess and notice which aspect might need a little more attention or enhancement. Coincidentally, you will notice what needs attention internally will be reflected in your external environment.

### To End

I would like to leave with you a question that I hope will spark the fire within to teach for a deeper purpose. What is the point of learning if not to become the best human being that we can be?

## REFERENCES


Graves, Donald H. 2001. *The Energy to Teach.* Page 35Portsmouth, NH: Heinemann.

Heiss, Renee. 2004. *Feng Shui for the Classroom.* Chicago, Illinois: Zephyr Press.

Healthy Child Healthy World. 2013. "8 Powerful Plants That Detox the Air In Your Home." https://www.mindbodygreen.com/0-12034/8-powerful-plants-that-can detox-the-air-in-your-home,html

Hoberman, Mary Ann. 1978. *A House is a House for Me.* Penguin Young Readers Group.

Immordino-Yang, Mary Helen. 2016. "Why Emotions Are Integral to Learning." https://ww2.kqed.org/mindshift/2016/05/31/why-emotions-are-integral-to-learning/

Lagatree, Kirsten M. 1998. *Feng Shui at Work.* New York: Random House Publishing.

Markman, Art. 2012. *Smart Thinking Three Essential Keys to Solve Problems, Innovate, and Get Things Done:* Penguin Group.

Mount-Cors, Mary Faith. 2008. "Bridging the differences: Cultural background of Mexican Students Entering U.S. Schools." https://www.learnnc.org/lp/editions/brdglangbarriers/4486

Scott, Elizabeth. 2017. "Everyday Mindfulness Exercises for Stress Relief." https://www.verywell.com/mindfulness-exercises-for-everyday-life-3145187

Routman, Regie. 2008. *Teaching Essentials.* Page 98 Portsmouth, NH: Heinemann.

Wagner, Saul. "Classroom Colors Make a Difference." https://www.hertzfurniture.com/buying-guide/classroom-design/classroom-colors.html

Wikipedia NASA Clean Air Study. 1989. https://en.wikipedia.org/wiki/NASA_Clean_Air_Study.

Wolfe, Pat. 1995. *How to Teach so Kids Will Learn: A Look at the Developmentally Appropriate Brain.* For Nellie Edge Seminars, Napa, CA.

# *About the Author*

*Bee Medders has over 25 years of experience in education as a primary teacher, literacy coordinator, staff developer, instructional coach, and mentor. She is currently working as a Program Consultant for the New Teacher Center. She received her teaching credential in 1990 at California State University, Hayward (now East Bay). In 1992, she received additional training in Developmentally Appropriate Practice and was trained as a Literacy Coordinator in 1997. Over the years, she has given workshops on room environment and has contributed to various publications. She is a proud recipient of numerous awards including the Margaret Lynch Area Exemplary Award Service for Outstanding Contribution to Reading in Area 3 from the California Reading Association, The David H. Russell Award for Excellence in Reading Instruction from the Alameda County Reading Association, and Certificate of Recognition from the Filipino American Education Association of California as Educator of the Year, PASE Chapter. Before becoming a teacher, Bee was a licensed Radiologic Technologist and graduated at Upstate Medical Center College of Health Related Professions in Syracuse, New York. She was born in the Philippines and grew up on the island of Guam before moving to New York. She resides in Castro Valley, California with her husband Mark, her daughter Lauren, their dog Kona, and her ninety-year old mother, Jovita, who was also a teacher of 22 years in the Philippines.*

To contact Bee for workshops or consultation,
send an email to
beemedders@gmail.com

Made in United States
Orlando, FL
26 June 2024

48307213R00031